The Spunky Coconut

Dairy-Free
ICE CREAM

- Soy-Free
- Sugar-Free
- Vegan

KELLY V. BROZYNA

Apidae Press · Longmont, Colorado

Apidae Press
www.ApidaePress.com

Text and Photography Copyright © Kelly V. Brozyna, 2012.
ISBN: 978-0-9827811-6-6 paperback
Library of Congress Control Number: 2012906547

This book is intended as a source of information only. The text and recipes should not be considered a substitute for professional medical expertise. The author disclaims any liability for any adverse effects arising from the application of the information found herein. The reader should consult a qualified health professional before starting any new diet or health program.

Visit www.TheSpunkyCoconut.com for additional recipes and articles.
Book design by Kelly and Andrew Brozyna, AJB Design, Inc., www.ajbdesign.com

Printed in the United States of America.

This book is dedicated to my readers.
Thank you so much for all your support,
and for helping me create this book.
Happy ice cream eating!

WITH GRATITUDE & LOVE

Thanks especially to my family who ate nothing but ice cream for a year, and who I could not have done this without. I love you Andy, Zoe, Ashley, and Ginger!

Thanks to my friend Lexie, of www.LexiesKitchen.com for all her love and support, and food photography props!

Thanks to my friends Elana Amsterdam, Aran Goyoaga, Amanda Hofeditz, Lisa Doran, Emily McNamera, and Becki Scott for all their love and support, and for inspiring me every day as a friend, mother, recipe developer and food photographer.

FOREWORD

When Kelly told me that she planned to write an ice cream book I became immediately interested in learning the history of frozen desserts. Much has been written on the charming history of ice cream, but the story of dairy-free ice cream is more obscure. I have written this brief essay to share with our casein-free, lactose intolerant, paleo, and vegan readers.

Various ancient cultures are known to have enjoyed flavored drinks mixed with ice shavings or snow. It was the development of a sixteenth century technique to artificially freeze food that allowed true ice creams and ices to be prepared in the kitchen. Mixing crushed ice with salt will produce a freezing effect. The specialized containers, tools, and training spread across Europe in the 1600s. Dairy-free ices and sorbets were all the rage with European aristocracy during the seventeenth and eighteenth centuries. The flavored ices were typically formed in elaborate molds and set as table centerpieces to delight dinner guests. French and Italian chefs became particularly known for their ices.

At the same time chefs were using their custard recipes to create milk-based ice creams. Interestingly, the very first ice cream cookbook discussed nut ingredients. In 1768 a Monsieur Emy printed an untitled book in which he described how to infuse the flavors of almonds and cashews into ice cream. Although this early chef lauded the taste and health benefits of nuts, before the twentieth century there seems to have been no interest in developing non-dairy nut-based ice creams. While ices have been prepared at home and sold commercially for as long as ice cream, it was the frozen treats made of dairy that went on to dominate the kitchen and the market.

At the end of the nineteenth century Ellen G. White preached against the large quantities of milk and sugar eaten by Americans. In the twentieth century members of her Seventh Day Adventist Church published some pioneering cookbooks advocating non-dairy ice cream recipes. In 1936 Adventist Dr. John Harvey Kellogg printed a soymilk ice cream recipe in his *Good Health* magazine. In the same year Dorothea Van Gundy self-published an Adventist cookbook *La Sierra Recipes* to promote her family's soy business. The book included vanilla, avocado-orange, and almond soy ice cream flavors.

Jethro Kloss included a single soymilk ice cream recipe in his 1939 best-selling cookbook *Back to Eden*. Kloss focused on soy as the preferred substitute for dairy, but his book mentioned that a milk could also be made from almonds. Dorothea Van Gundy published another book in 1963. *The Soy Bean Cookbook* featured five soy ice creams.

In 1968 *The Ten Talents* was perhaps the first published cookbook to include nut-based ice creams. Authors Frank and Rosalie Hurd developed ice cream recipes reliant on almonds, cashews, and coconut. Hundreds of thousands of copies of *The Soy Bean Cookbook* were sold. *Back to Eden* and *The Ten Talents* sold equally well, and they are still in print.

Seventh-day Adventists have avoided milk to support good health, an important point in their theology. The Jewish community has served dairy-free iced treats as part of its own religious observance. Kosher laws forbid the consumption of dairy and meat in the same meal. Eating a dairy ice cream even a few hours after a hamburger could be a no-no, so ices have long filled the role of frozen dessert. Several companies in 1920s New York City sold kosher dairy ice cream (to be eaten away from meats). They quickly started offering dairy-free ices as well. Eggs were used as a way to create a creamy texture, but these were replaced by soy lecithin in the early 1940s. In the later 1940s Jewish caterers, ice cream shops, and housewives were using the first commercially available soy-based whipped topping to create non-dairy ice creams.

Early interest in soy wasn't limited to religious groups. The above-mentioned Rich's Whip Topping was developed using soymilk research conducted by Henry Ford. It maybe surprising to learn that the founder of the Ford Motor company had a personal interest in soy beans. In the early 1930s he built a soymilk plant and collected scientists to study soy bean's commercial potential. At the 1934 Chicago World's Fair, Ford's exhibit sold experimental tofu ice cream. World War II forced

Ford's program to abandon its soy food research, but their discoveries influenced future soy ice cream makers. In 1945, health food advocate Mildred Lager published *The Useful Soybean*, which offered a soymilk/coconut milk ice cream recipe. Lager's unpublished soymilk ice cream recipes were later adapted by Dorothea Van Gundy for her 1963 *Soy Bean Cookbook*.

Many state legislatures had regulations which made it difficult for the dairy-free ventures to get started. For instance, until 1968 dairy-free ice creams weren't officially allowed to be sold in New York because of the technicality that there was no existing legal standard to follow. Until 1976 California's department of agriculture would not allow non-dairy ice cream to be sold in soft-serve machines. Careful petitioning by ice cream producers across the country quickly opened the legality for their new dairy-free products. It is interesting to note that the word "ice cream" is not allowed on today's packaging of commercially sold dairy-free desserts. State departments of agriculture require the less romantic term, "Non-Dairy Frozen Dessert".

In the following decades popular interest in the vegetarian diet, the vegan diet, and overall healthy eating grew. Dairy-free ice cream became more common, but the recipes continued to depend on soy. While soymilk creates a great texture for ice cream, it comes with a variety of problems. Soy is difficult to digest, mucus-forming, and it contains phytoestrogens which influence a person's hormonal balance. Soy plants grown in the United States are most often genetically modified organisms. Many people suffer from an allergy to soy.

Around the turn of the century, raw foodists began promoting dairy-free recipes that are consciously soy-free. *Raw: The Uncookbook* (1999) by Juliano Brotman included three frozen treats—gelato, ice cream, and a torte. All were based on blended nuts, nut butter, coconut, or fruit. A flurry of raw books by other authors appeared in the 2000s, which often included similarly-prepared ice cream recipes.

In the twenty-first century popular interest in dairy-free ice cream is at its height. The trail-blazing Adventist food community and the early-adopting kosher community have been joined by vegans, raw foodists, paleo dieters, the casein intolerant, lactose intolerant, and the generally health conscious. Today's health food markets commonly carry ice creams made of coconut milk, hemp milk, rice milk, and soy milk. In recent years a flurry of devoted non-dairy shops have opened, delighting the dairy-free crowd in cities across the US and Europe.

The Spunky Coconut Dairy-Free Ice Cream Cookbook takes the best from each of these historic dairy-free ice cream traditions. The recipes in this book feature an ice cream base of coconut and nuts, but Kelly's particular method doesn't require the time and expense of strict raw food preparation. Her ice creams avoid the problematic soy of Adventist and vegan cookbooks, but take advantage of their concept of using a non-dairy milk for smooth texture. In addition to original flavors, Kelly provides old favorites that you would expect from a conventional dairy ice cream cookbook. She accomplishes the right sweetness without the customarily enormous amounts of unhealthy white sugar. I'm sure you will enjoy Kelly's innovative contribution the library of dairy-free ice cream cookbooks.

Cheers,
Andrew Brozyna

FURTHER READING

Aoyagi, Akiko and Shurtleff, William. *Tofutti & Other Soy Ice Creams: The Non-Dairy Frozen Dessert Industry and Trade*. Lafayette, CA: The Soyfoods Center, 1989.

Day, Ivan. *Ice Cream*. Oxford: Shire Publications, 2011.

Quinzio, Jeri. *Of Sugar and Snow: A History of Ice Cream Making.* Berkely: University of Califronia Press, 2009.

INTRODUCTION

Hi! I'm Kelly, and I'm so excited to share this dairy-free ice cream cookbook with you! As you may know from my first two cookbooks and my website TheSpunkyCoconut.com I'm *crazy* about ice cream. I've been experimenting with dairy-free ice cream for many years now, and I'm putting everything I've learned here in this cookbook. I hope you enjoy it as much as my family and I do!

The Tools

BLENDER AND ICE CREAM MACHINE

The recipes in this cookbook call for about one quart of ice cream, because the most common and affordable ice cream machines are one quart sized, and so are most blenders. I highly recommend a professional blender, like a Blendtec (my personal preference), to get the best results. I've been using my Blendtec at least once a day for many years, and after comparing it to other similarly priced blenders - it is the best. Blendtecs fit on your counter under the upper cabinets, have the most power, and are easier to clean, just to name a few reasons why they're better. I have an affiliate link to Blendtecs on TheSpunkyCoconut.com, so if you decide to purchase one please go through me—I really appreciate it!

My ice cream machine is a Cuisinart, and I have an affiliate link to that on TheSpunkyCoconut.com too. I bought an extra freezer bowl for it, which I keep in my basement freezer trunk so that I always have one ready to go. *The bowls must be in the freezer for 24 hours or more, before they are ready to make ice cream.* The only downside is that my model (which is not the most recent) is very loud. But I just run it in the basement so it isn't that big a deal. *Whatever machine you choose, be sure to read all of the manufacturers instructions first.*

SIX CUP RECTANGULAR GLASS DISH WITH A LID

I like to use a six cup rectangular glass dish with a lid to freeze my ice cream in the freezer (as seen on p. 14). Plastic transfers toxins to your food and drinks, plus it breaks, holds odors, and is a bad choice for the environment. The shallow design of the six cup rectangular glass dish helps the ice cream freeze faster and defrost more evenly than a deep dish (like a bread loaf pan). I get mine at the local Ace Hardware store, but you can also find them on Amazon.

SPOONULA

One of the most important pieces of equipment is also one of the least expensive—a flexible silicone spatula, or "spoonula". This is the tool you need to get your ice cream out of the ice cream machine freezer bowl without scratching and damaging its inner surface. The ice cream often freezes too tightly to the walls of the bowl, so that you can't get this outer coating of ice cream out until it melts for an hour or so. Don't worry, just remove the ice cream in the middle of the ice cream machine bowl, then wait until that shell has softened to transfer it to the dish.

ICE CREAM SCOOP WITH A LEVER

Of course you can get your ice cream out without the use of an ice cream scoop with a lever, but I had to mention this useful tool just in case you're wondering how to get a pretty scoop. It makes getting a nice scoop so much easier, and I use mine for other recipes too, like scooping muffin batter into paper cups.

ICE POP MOLDS

We love to make ice cream pops all year (and especially pudding pops for breakfast, p. 69). The fastest and easiest way to make them is with a kit. We use Tovolo Groovy Ice Pop Molds because they're BPA-Free. I bought them on Amazon.

The Ingredients

COCONUT MILK

My ice creams are based primarily on full-fat coconut milk. I use Thai Kitchen because it is the richest coconut milk, but it does contain a very small amount of guar gum. (Use another brand, like Natural Value, if you want to be 100% gum-free.) I combine coconut milk with cashew milk, hemp milk, or coconut water (I prefer Amy & Brian coconut juice) so that the coconut flavor doesn't overpower the ice cream.

CASHEW MILK & HEMP MILK

Cashew milk and hemp milk are my favorite dairy-free milks to combine with coconut milk. I suggest two options because some of you will prefer using homemade cashew milk (which is completely gum-free) while others will prefer buying hemp milk. The nice thing about buying hemp milk is that it's ready to go when you have a sudden urge to make ice cream—there's no waiting or blending. However, if you prefer making cashew milk, you will be amazed at how easy it is to do. *And of course you can substitute another non-dairy beverage if you like.*

♥ I use Unsweetened Vanilla, Living Harvest Tempt hemp milk

♥ To make cashew milk simply cover one cup of plain cashews (not roasted or seasoned) with water, plus two inches, and let the cashews soak overnight. In the morning strain the cashews (dispose of the soaking water - it contains enzymes which inhibit digestion) and blend with about four cups of fresh water. That's it. No need to strain like when making almond milk. Also, I've found over the years that cashew milk lasts longer than almond milk in the fridge. I keep mine for five days or longer.

There are several options for sweeteners. Whichever sweetener you choose, there are about one to two tablespoons per serving (using six servings per recipe in this book). If you want to reduce the total sugar in a recipe further, then cut the ingredient in half and substitute extra milk and stevia. For instance, *if a recipe calls for ½ cup honey you can substitute with ¼ cup honey, ¼ cup coconut milk, and ¼ teaspoon (or more as desired) liquid stevia.* NuNaturals and NOW Foods are our favorite stevia brands these days.

- ▾ **Honey:** Local honey is a natural sweetener that has been reported to help with allergies. It is not very low glycemic index, but it does contain minerals, vitamins, amino acids, and antioxidants. ***Honey is not vegan.***

- ▾ **Agave:** Raw agave is the healthiest form of agave, although it is still arguable as to whether or not it is healthy. This debate is due to the form of sugar found in agave: fructose. Agave is low glycemic index and vegan.

- ▾ **Dates:** Dates (or bananas) are natural sweeteners, as well as natural thickeners. They will effect the color and flavor of the recipes. They are not very low glycemic index.

- ▾ **Coconut sugar:** Coconut sugar is an unrefined, low glycemic sugar. It comes from the sap of the flowering branch of coconut trees. Once the branch is tapped, the sap flows for 20 years, making it extremely sustainable. *You can substitute any other granulated sugar in equal amounts if that is what you prefer.*

- ▾ **Stevia:** Stevia is an herb that is zero on the glycemic index. I use stevia in combination with honey/agave/coconut sugar. This allows me to keep the sugar to a fraction of the amount found in traditional recipes. We prefer NuNaturals and NOW Foods vanilla liquid stevia these days.

We prefer the texture of these ice creams with thickener, *especially when I plan on storing the ice cream, as opposed to eating it right away*. The guar gum will keep it softer straight from the freezer, often requiring only about ten minutes on the counter before scooping. However, *all thickeners are optional*. If you prefer to add thickeners too, then I highly recommend including one from the list below so that your ice cream feels more smooth. There are several options:

♥ **Option 1:** Add ½ teaspoon guar gum.
Guar gum is the best way to thicken these dairy-free ice creams. I prefer guar gum to xanthan gum for two reasons. First, I prefer that guar gum comes from guar or "cluster beans," while xanthan gum comes from bacteria. And two, I prefer guar gum, because xanthan gum bothers a lot of people (possibly due to the fact that it's usually grown on corn). *There are about six servings in each of these batches of ice cream, which means that there is less than ⅛ teaspoon of guar gum per serving.*

♥ **Option 2:** Add 1 tablespoon gelatin.
The gelatin needs to be completely dissolved in ¼ cup boiling water. Pour it in last, just before you puree the ice cream mixture. This was the first technique I used to thicken my dairy-free ice creams. It works well, but not as well as guar gum. Gelatin is healing to the gut and is allowed on Paleo and GAPS diets, but **it is not vegetarian or vegan**.

♥ **Option 3:** Substitute ½ cup dates for the honey or agave in the recipe.
Dates are good at thickening, but not as good as guar gum or gelatin. Also, dates will effect the color of the ice cream. You can use very ripe bananas too, but they will of course add banana flavor.

Cool Tips

- Although it doesn't add as much air as commercial ice cream machine, your home ice cream maker does add air and volume.

- *To get a pretty scoop* you need to freeze your ice cream until it's hard, which means taking it from the ice cream machine to the freezer.

- Let your homemade ice cream defrost for ten to twenty minutes before scooping.

- The less sweetener you use, the harder your ice cream will freeze.

- The more you thaw and refreeze your ice cream the more icy it will become.

- Keep an empty glass storage container in the freezer. That way, when you put the freshly made ice cream into the frozen container it won't melt as much.

- I use Tovolo Groovy Ice Pop Molds, because their plastic is BPA-free.

CLASSICS

Bing Cherry Ice Cream

I have a passion for Bing cherries and cherry cordials. This ice cream combines those two flavors making it one of my absolute favorites. So when you see Bing cherries in season, grab them. And add a little Olive Nation amaretto extract to really make it pop.

INGREDIENTS

amaretto extract *(I use Olive Nation)* · Bing cherries · cashew milk or hemp milk *(p. 3)* · coconut milk *(canned full-fat)* · guar gum *(or other thickener, p. 5)* · honey or raw agave · lemon juice · vanilla extract

Add to high power blender or food processor:

1 cup pitted Bing cherries

1½ cups coconut milk

1 cup cashew milk or hemp milk

½ cup honey or raw agave

1 tsp lemon juice

1 tsp vanilla extract

¼ tsp amaretto extract

½ tsp guar gum

Puree until creamy and smooth.

Freeze for about an hour or refrigerate until cold. Pour into ice cream machine, per manufacturers instructions.

Optional: Add another cup finely chopped pitted cherries when the ice cream is soft serve consistency.

Eat straight from ice cream machine or freeze until hard for pretty scoops *(p. 6)*.

Blueberry Lavender Ice Cream

This is one of those flavors that had I never heard of, until one of you told me about it. Thank you so much—we love it! And the color is so pretty and fun too.

INGREDIENTS

blueberries · cashew milk or hemp milk *(p. 3)* · coconut milk *(canned full-fat)* · guar gum *(or other thickener, p. 5)* · honey or raw agave · lavender · lemon juice · vanilla extract

---

Add to high power blender or food processor:
- 1 cup fresh blueberries
- 2 cups coconut milk
- ½ tsp lavender

Puree until creamy and smooth.

Add:
- 1 cup cashew milk or hemp milk
- ½ cup honey or raw agave
- 1 tsp lemon juice
- 2 tsp vanilla extract
- ½ tsp guar gum

Puree until creamy and smooth.

Freeze for about an hour or refrigerate until cold. Pour into ice cream machine, per manufacturers instructions.

Eat straight from ice cream machine or freeze until hard for pretty scoops *(p. 6)*.

Butter Pecan Ice Cream

Butter Pecan has always been one of my favorite flavors of ice cream. Who doesn't love anything buttery, really?

INGREDIENTS

cashew milk or hemp milk *(p. 3)* · coconut milk *(canned full-fat)* · Earth Balance Buttery Spread *(I use soy-free)* · guar gum *(or other thickener, p. 5)* · honey or raw agave · pecan pieces · sea salt · vanilla extract

Toast 1½ cups of pecan pieces at 350°F for about ten minutes. While it's still hot from the oven add:

    2 tbsp Earth Balance Buttery Spread

    ¼ tsp sea salt

Combine then chill in the fridge.

Add to high power blender or food processor:

    2 cups coconut milk

    1¼ cups cashew milk or hemp milk

    ½ cup honey or agave

    5 tbsp Earth Balance Buttery Spread

    2 tsp vanilla extract

    ½ tsp guar gum

Puree until creamy and smooth.

Freeze for about an hour or refrigerate until cold. Pour into ice cream machine, per manufacturers instructions.

Add the pecans when the ice cream is soft serve consistency. Eat straight from ice cream machine or freeze until hard for pretty scoops *(p. 6)*.

Note: This flavor takes much longer to freeze because of the Earth Balance Buttery Spread.

Chocolate Ice Cream

My chocolate ice cream is extra creamy because I use dates and guar gum. If two thickeners is too indulgent for you, then you can always leave out the guar gum.

INGREDIENTS
cashew milk or hemp milk *(p. 3)* · cocoa or raw cacao powder · coconut milk *(canned full-fat)* · guar gum *(or other thickener, p. 5)* · medjool dates · vanilla extract

Add to high power blender or food processor:
   2 cups coconut milk
   10 pitted dates *(soaked first if they are dry)*
Puree until smooth.

Add:
   1 cup cashew milk or hemp milk
   ⅓ cup cocoa or raw cacao powder
   1 tbsp vanilla extract
   ½ tsp guar gum
Puree until creamy and smooth.

Freeze for about an hour or refrigerate
until cold. Pour into ice cream machine, per
manufacturers instructions.

Eat straight from ice cream machine or freeze
until hard for pretty scoops *(p. 6)*.

Chocolate Hazelnut Ice Cream

INGREDIENTS

Chocolate Hazelnut Spread *(p. 16)* · Chocolate Ice Cream base *(p. 13)*

Make Chocolate Hazelnut Spread.

Make Chocolate Ice Cream.

Add to high power blender or food processor:
   All of the Chocolate Ice Cream base
   2 tbsp Chocolate Hazelnut Spread
Puree until creamy and smooth.

Freeze for about two hours or refrigerate
until cold. Pour into ice cream machine, per
manufacturers instructions.

Spread the ice cream in the dish.

Fold in chunks of Chocolate Hazelnut Spread
as seen opposite. Freeze until hard for pretty
scoops *(p. 6)*.

Chocolate Hazelnut Spread

The first time I had chocolate hazelnut spread was when I visited Rome in my early 20's. I ordered it on a fresh hot crepe—a common treat in Italy and other parts of Europe. My eyes bugged out of my head as I devoured the plate-full. Many years later I had to recreate chocolate hazelnut spread to be healthier with a third of the sugar and no dairy. I'm sure you will love it too.

INGREDIENTS

coconut milk *(canned full-fat)* · coconut sugar · dairy-free dark chocolate *(I use Chocolove 70%)* · hazelnuts · sea salt

Toast 1½ cups of hazelnuts at 350°F for about 15 minutes.

While they're toasting, heat in a small pan:
   1½ cups coconut milk
   ½ cup coconut sugar
   ⅛ tsp sea salt
When the sugar is melted remove it from the heat.

Meanwhile, melt over double boiler:
   3 bars (3.2 oz each) of dark chocolate

Remove the toasted hazelnuts from the oven and let them cool slightly. Transfer them to a clean dry kitchen towel. Rub the hazelnuts in the towel to remove as much of the skin as possible. Add them to your food processor.

Puree until the hazelnuts are very fine. Add the melted chocolate bars. Puree until creamy and smooth *(about two minutes)*. While still pureeing add the milk mixture. Puree until smooth.

Note: Readers have tried my chocolate hazelnut spread with even darker chocolate than I suggest, and reported problems. Stick to 70% dark chocolate or lower, and order the brand I use, Chocolove, if you want to make extra sure to get the same results. Amazon sells Chocolove for a great price.

Hazelnut

Eggnog Ice Cream

INGREDIENTS
allspice · cinnamon · nutmeg · Vanilla Ice Cream base *(p. 34)*

Make Vanilla Ice Cream base.

Add:
    ¾ tsp cinnamon
    ¾ tsp nutmeg
    ¼ tsp allspice
Puree until creamy and smooth.

Freeze for about two hours or refrigerate
until cold. Pour into ice cream machine, per
manufacturers instructions.

Eat straight from ice cream machine or freeze
until hard for pretty scoops *(p. 6)*.

See www.TheSpunkyCoconut.com for an eggnog
recipe that contains eggs.

Fig Ice Cream

Figs add fantastic texture to this ice cream. I tried using them soaked but raw, however, they are so much more amazing after cooking slightly. If you're a fan of figs, you will love this ice cream.

INGREDIENTS

cashew or hemp milk *(p. 3)* · coconut milk *(canned full-fat)* · coconut sugar · Earth Balance Buttery Spread *(I use soy-free)* · figs · guar gum *(or other thickener, p. 5)* · lemon juice · sea salt · vanilla extract

Soak 30 dry figs (about half a pound) in a cup water overnight. The next day discard the soaking water, remove the stems, and cut each fig in half.

Add the figs to a pan preheated over low/medium heat with two tablespoons Earth Balance Buttery Spread and two teaspoons of lemon juice.

Reduce heat to low, cover and cook about ten minutes, stirring occasionally, and mashing them down.

Add to food processor:
    cooked figs
    2 cups coconut milk
    1 cup cashew or hemp milk
    2 tbsp coconut sugar
    1 tbsp vanilla extract
    pinch sea salt
    ½ tsp guar gum
Puree until creamy and smooth.

Freeze for about two hours or refrigerate until cold. Pour into ice cream machine, per manufacturers instructions.

Eat straight from ice cream machine or freeze until hard for pretty scoops *(p. 6)*.

Mint Chocolate Swirl Ice Cream

Mint Chocolate Chip was one of my two favorite flavors as a child. (The other was Rocky Road.) I gave it a twist by using a fudge swirl or ganache topping, and I think it's even better. If you prefer you can add chocolate chips instead.

INGREDIENTS

coconut milk *(canned full-fat)* · dairy-free chocolate chips *(I use Enjoy Life)* · spearmint extract *(I use Frontier Organic Mint Flavor)* · Vanilla Ice Cream base *(p. 34)*

GANACHE:

Add to bowl:
⅓ cup dairy-free chocolate chips

Heat ⅓ cup coconut milk until it just begins to simmer. Pour hot coconut milk over chips to melt them. Stir to combine. Set aside.

Optional: Add ¼ tsp alchohol-free spearmint extract OR a few drops of peppermint extract.

ICE CREAM:

Make Vanilla Ice Cream base

Add:
1 tsp of alchohol-free spearmint extract
OR ¼ to ½ tsp of peppermint extract

Optional: To make the ice cream green add equal parts of blue and yellow India Tree natural food coloring.

Puree until creamy and smooth. Freeze for about one hour or refrigerate until cold. Pour into ice cream machine, per manufacturers instructions.

Add homemade ganache to your mint ice cream. Top ice cream with ganache OR mix ganache into ice cream before putting it in the freezer.

Freeze until hard for pretty scoops *(p. 6)*.

Pecan Praline Ice Cream

INGREDIENTS

cashew milk *or* hemp milk *(p. 3)* · coconut milk *(canned full-fat)* · coconut sugar *(p. 4)* · Earth Balance Buttery Spread *(I use soy-free)* · guar gum *(or other thickener, p. 5)* · honey or raw agave · pecans · vanilla extract · water

Pre-heat a medium sized pan over low to medium heat.

Add:
   2 tbsp Earth Balance Buttery Spread
   2 tbsp water
   ¾ cup coconut sugar
   2¼ cups pecans
Simmer gently for about 5 - 10 minutes, until the sugar is melted and slightly thickened. Pour candied pecans onto unbleached parchment paper to cool.

Add to blender or food processor:
   ⅓ cup of the candied pecans
   2 cups coconut milk
   1 cup cashew or hemp milk
   2 tbsp honey or raw agave (or more
      as desired)
   1 tsp vanilla extract
   ½ tsp guar gum
Puree until creamy and smooth.

Freeze for about two hours or refrigerate until cold. Pour into ice cream machine, per manufacturers instructions. Add the rest of the candied pecans to ice cream when it is soft serve consistency.

Eat straight from ice cream machine or freeze until hard for pretty scoops *(p. 6)*.

Pińa Colada Ice Cream

INGREDIENTS
coconut cream · guar gum *(or other thickener, p. 5)* · honey or raw agave · pineapple ·
rum · vanilla extract

Add to high power blender or food processor:

2½ cups coconut cream*

¼ cup honey or raw agave

1¼ cups sliced pineapple

1 tsp vanilla extract

½ tsp guar gum

Optional: 2 tbsp rum

Puree until creamy and smooth.

Freeze for about an hour or refrigerate
until cold. Pour into ice cream machine, per
manufacturers instructions.

Eat straight from ice cream machine or freeze
until hard for pretty scoops *(p. 6)*.

*To get coconut cream put a few cans of full-
fat coconut milk *(I use Thai Kitchen)* in the
refrigerator over night to get it to separate.
Open the can and scoop the cream off of the top.

Pistachio Ice Cream

Pistachio was the first ice cream flavor we tested for this book, and it made it's way onto the cover. The girls especially, loved it so much that I knew we were going to have a blast making The Spunky Coconut ice cream book.

INGREDIENTS

almond extract · cashew milk or hemp milk *(p. 3)* · coconut milk *(canned full-fat)* · Earth Balance Buttery Spread *(I use soy-free)* · guar gum *(or other thickener, p. 5)* · honey or raw agave · unsalted roasted pistachios · vanilla extract

Add to food processor:

    1 cup unsalted roasted pistachios

    ½ cup honey or raw agave

Puree until almost butter, scraping the sides as necessary while pureeing.

Add to the pistachio puree:

    2 cups coconut milk

    1¼ cups cashew milk or hemp milk

    1 tbsp Earth Balance Buttery Spread

    1 tsp vanilla extract

    ½ tsp guar gum

    sea salt (to taste)

    Optional: ⅛ to ¼ tsp almond extract

Puree until creamy and smooth.

Freeze for about two hours or refrigerate until cold. Pour into ice cream machine, per manufacturers instructions.

Eat straight from ice cream machine or freeze until hard for pretty scoops *(p. 6)*.

Pumpkin Ice Cream

INGREDIENTS

cashew milk or hemp milk *(p. 3)* · coconut milk *(canned full-fat)* · guar gum *(or other thickener, p. 5)* · honey or raw agave · pumpkin pie spice · pumpkin puree · vanilla extract

Add to high power blender or food processor:

1 cup pumpkin puree

1½ cups coconut milk

1 cup cashew milk or hemp milk

½ cup honey or raw agave

1 tsp vanilla extract

½ tsp pumpkin pie spice

½ tsp guar gum

Puree until creamy and smooth.

Freeze for about two hours or refrigerate until cold. Pour into ice cream machine, per manufacturers instructions.

Eat straight from ice cream machine or freeze until hard for pretty scoops *(p. 6)*.

Roasted Banana Ice Cream

Sauteed bananas are so amazing, and of course the butter substitute only makes everything even better. Yum.

INGREDIENTS

bananas · cashew or hemp milk *(p. 3)* · coconut milk *(canned full-fat)* · coconut sugar · Earth Balance Buttery Spread *(I use soy-free)* · guar gum *(or other thickener, p. 5)* · lemon juice · vanilla extract · water

Slice 2 medium-size bananas into ½ inch pieces. Saute banana slices in 2 tablespoons of Earth Balance Buttery Spread, using a pan that has been pre-heated over low/medium heat.

When the bananas are brown on both sides add them to high power blender or food processor, making sure to get all the brown bits. Let the pan cool then put it back on the burner over low heat.

Add to the pan:
   ¼ cup + 2 tbsp coconut sugar
   2 tbsp water
When the sugar is just dissolved add it to the blender or food processor with the bananas.

Also add to the blender or food processor:
   2½ cups coconut milk
   1 cup cashew or hemp milk
   2 tsp vanilla extract

   2 tsp lemon juice
   ½ tsp guar gum
Puree until creamy and smooth.

Freeze for about two hours or refrigerate until cold. Pour into ice cream machine, per manufacturers instructions.

Eat straight from ice cream machine or freeze until hard for pretty scoops *(p. 6)*.

Rocky Road Ice Cream

The chocolate ice cream, crunchy nuts and gooey marshmallow cream were what I loved about Rocky Road as a child. And I still do.

INGREDIENTS
Chocolate Ice Cream base *(p. 13)* · marshmallow · toasted walnuts

Make Chocolate Ice Cream base

Freeze for about two hours or refrigerate until cold. Pour into ice cream machine, per manufacturers instructions. Add 1 cup chopped toasted walnuts to ice cream when it is soft serve consistency.

Fold in Suzanne's vegan RiceMellow Creme *(www.suzannes-specialties.com)*.

Eat right away or freeze until hard for pretty scoops *(p. 6)*.

Optional: If you are ***not*** vegan/vegetarian I highly recommend you try Honey Marshmallow Fluff:

HONEY MARSHMALLOW FLUFF
Based on Honey Marshmallows by Jenni Wiehoff-Hulet. Check out all of Jenni's great recipes on UrbanPoser.blogspot.com

Add to a medium/large deep mixing bowl:
   ½ cup water
   1 tbsp beef gelatin *(I order mine on iHerb.com)*
   1 tsp vanilla extract
   ¼ tsp sea salt
Set aside.

Add to a small pot:
   ½ cup water
   1 cup honey
Bring to simmer.

Simmer until you reach 240°F degrees on the candy thermometer. Carefully pour into bowl with water, gelatin, vanilla, and salt. Beat with handheld mixer or stand mixer for about eight minutes, when it will be fluffy, white, and almost doubled in size! Store at room temperature in a glass container with a lid.

Rum Raisin Ice Cream

The first ever cookbook devoted to ice cream was written by the French chef Monsieur Emy in 1768. Emy was opposed to alcohol as an ingredient, but he reluctantly made an exception for rum. Later 18th and 19th century chefs enthusiastically embraced rum for their ice creams. —Andrew

INGREDIENTS

Vanilla Ice Cream base *(p. 34)* · raisins · dark rum

Add to a small bowl:
  ½ cup raisins
  ½ cup dark rum

Soak raisins in rum overnight. Strain the raisins and reserve 2 tablespoons of the rum for the ice cream.

Make Vanilla Ice Cream base.

Add 1 to 2 tablespoons of the reserved rum to the vanilla ice cream mixture.

Freeze for about two hours or refrigerate until cold. Pour into ice cream machine, per manufacturers instructions.

Add rum-soaked raisins to ice cream when it is soft serve consistency.

Optional: This flavor is also nice with some ground nutmeg. Add nutmeg to your taste.

Eat straight from ice cream machine or freeze until hard for pretty scoops *(p. 6)*.

Strawberry Ice Cream

Strawberry ice cream is one of the most popular flavors among children. I know it's delicious, and so summery, but I can't help wonder, is it also the pink color that makes them so happy?

INGREDIENTS
cashew milk or hemp milk *(p. 3)* · coconut milk *(canned full-fat)* · guar gum *(or other thickener, p. 5)* · honey or raw agave · lemon juice · strawberries · vanilla extract

Add to high power blender or food processor:
    2 cups of strawberries (or about 10 ounces)
    1½ cups coconut milk
    1 cup cashew milk or hemp milk
    ½ cup honey or raw agave
    2 tsp vanilla extract
    1 tsp lemon juice
    ½ tsp guar gum
Puree until creamy and smooth.

Freeze for about one hour or refrigerate
until cold. Pour into ice cream machine, per
manufacturers instructions.

Optional: Add finely chopped fresh
strawberries to ice cream when it is soft serve
consistency.

Eat straight from ice cream machine or freeze
until hard for pretty scoops *(p. 6)*.

Sunbutter Fudge Ripple Ice Cream

INGREDIENTS

cashew milk or hemp milk *(p. 3)* · dairy-free chocolate chips · coconut milk *(canned full-fat)* · medjool dates · guar gum *(or other thickener, p. 5)* · sea salt · SunButter · vanilla extract

GANACHE:

Add to bowl:

⅓ cup dairy-free chocolate chips

Heat ⅓ cup coconut milk until it just begins to simmer. Pour hot coconut milk over chips to melt them. Stir to combine. Set aside.

ICE CREAM

Add to high power blender or food processor:

2 cups coconut milk
½ cup soft pitted medjool dates *(soaked first if they are dry)*

Puree until creamy and smooth.

Add:

1½ cups cashew milk or hemp milk
¼ cup SunButter (sunflower seed butter)
pinch sea salt
1 tbsp vanilla extract
½ tsp guar gum

Puree until creamy and smooth.

Freeze for about one hour or refrigerate until cold. Pour into ice cream machine, per manufacturers instructions.

Layer with ganache. Freeze until hard for pretty scoops *(p. 6)*.

Swiss Almond Ice Cream

Swiss almond ice cream is so simple, but so satisfying. The contrast of sweet and salty, smooth and crunchy, is what makes it so appealing.

INGREDIENTS
Vanilla Ice Cream base *(p. 34)* · almond extract · almonds · dairy-free chocolate chips
· sea salt

Toast 1 cup of almonds at 350°F for about 12 minutes.

Add hot toasted almonds to a bowl that contains ½ cup dairy-free chocolate chips and ¼ tsp sea salt.

Cover the almonds, chocolate and sea salt for about two minutes so that the heat melts the chocolate. Stir to coat the almonds in the melted chocolate. Spread the coated almonds on unbleached parchment paper and chill. Chop the chocolate covered almonds when the chocolate is dry and cool.

Make Vanilla Ice Cream base.

Add ¼ tsp almond extract to the vanilla ice cream mixture.

Freeze for about one hour or refrigerate until cold. Pour into ice cream machine, per manufacturers instructions. Add chopped chocolate covered almonds to ice cream when it is soft serve consistency.

Eat straight from ice cream machine or freeze until hard for pretty scoops *(p. 6)*.

Toasted Coconut Ice Cream

cashew milk or hemp milk *(p. 3)* · coconut milk *(canned full-fat)* · shredded unsweetened coconut · guar gum *(or other thickener, p. 5)* · honey, agave, or coconut sugar · sea salt · vanilla extract

Add 1½ cups of shredded unsweetened coconut to a large casserole dish.

Add the dish to a pre-heated 350°F oven. Toast the coconut for about 8 minutes, stirring every few minutes, until it is golden colored.

Add to a medium sized pot:
  2½ cups coconut milk
  1 cup cashew milk or hemp milk
  the toasted shredded coconut from above
Bring to a simmer, watching carefully so it doesn't boil over.

Turn the heat off, put the lid on and steep for about 1 hour. Strain the shredded coconut for a perfectly smooth ice cream. Leave the shredded coconut in for a coarse ice cream texture.

Add to high power blender or food processor:
  liquids from above
  ⅓ cup honey, raw agave, or coconut sugar
  2 tsp vanilla extract
  pinch of sea salt
  more coconut milk until you have a total of
    four cups of liquids
  ½ tsp guar gum
Puree until creamy and smooth.

Freeze or refrigerate until cold. Pour into ice cream machine, per manufacturers instructions.

Eat straight from ice cream machine or freeze until hard for pretty scoops *(p. 6)*.

.ce Cream

mp milk *(p. 3)* · coconut milk *(canned full-fat)* · guar gum *(or other*
.oney or raw agave · vanilla extract

Add to high power blender or food processor:
  2 cups coconut milk
  1½ cups cashew milk or hemp milk
  ½ honey or raw agave
  1 tbsp vanilla extract
  ½ tsp guar gum
Puree until creamy and smooth.

Freeze for an hour or refrigerate until cold.
Pour into ice cream machine, per manufacturers
instructions.

Eat straight from ice cream machine or freeze
until hard for pretty scoops *(p. 6)*.

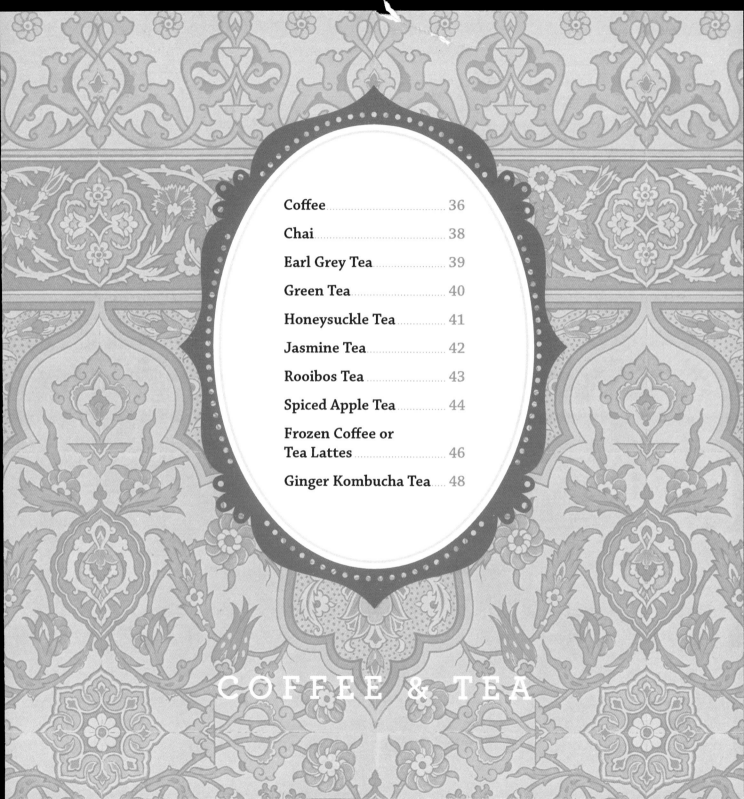

COFFEE & TEA

Coffee Ice Cream

Using coffee as an ingredient is similar to cooking with wine. You have to use a good quality coffee or wine, for a nice end result. Our favorite coffee comes from Red Frog Coffee. It's roasted locally, organic, fair trade and delicious.

INGREDIENTS

cashew milk or hemp milk *(p. 3)* · coconut milk *(canned full-fat)* · coffee beans · guar gum *(or other thickener, p. 5)* · honey or raw agave · vanilla extract · water

Grind ¼ cup organic coffee beans in a coffee grinder or Magic Bullet. Add grinds to a French press. Add 1 cup of water, just off the boil. Steep about ten minutes. Press the coffee grinds down then pour the coffee into the blender or food processor.

Add:
    2 cups coconut milk
    1 cup cashew milk or hemp milk
    ½ cup honey or raw agave
    2 tsp vanilla extract
    ½ tsp guar gum
Puree until creamy and smooth.

Freeze for about two hours or refrigerate until cold. Pour into ice cream machine, per manufacturers instructions.

Eat straight from ice cream machine or freeze until hard for pretty scoops *(p. 6)*.

Coffee ice cream shown opposite with chocolate candy from *(p. 73)* poured on top.

Mocha Almond Fudge

Make coffee ice cream. Freeze for about two hours or refrigerate until cold. Pour into ice cream machine, per manufacturers instructions.

Add 1 cup chopped toasted almonds to ice cream when it is soft serve consistency.

Layer with ganache *(p. 30)*. Freeze until hard for pretty scoops *(p. 6)*.

Chai Ice Cream

Chai is my favorite hot tea. I make this chai ice cream the same way—with coconut milk and honey.

INGREDIENTS

cashew milk or hemp milk *(p. 3)* · coconut milk *(canned full-fat)* · decaf chai spice *(I like Stash Decaf Chai Spice and Celestial Seasonings Chai Tea, Decaf India Spice)* · guar gum *(or other thickener, p. 5)* · honey or raw agave · water · vanilla extract

---

Add to medium sized pot:

    2¼ cups coconut milk
    1 cup cashew milk or hemp milk
    ¾ cup water
    3 tbsp + 1 tsp chai

Bring to a simmer, watching carefully so it doesn't boil over. Turn off the heat, put the lid on and steep for about 20 minutes. Remove the lid and let the mixture cool. Strain the tea from the liquid.

Add to high power blender or food processor:

    strained liquid
    ½ cup honey or raw agave
    1 tsp vanilla extract
    ½ tsp guar gum

Puree until creamy and smooth.

Freeze for about two hours or refrigerate until cold. Pour into ice cream machine, per manufacturers instructions.

Eat straight from ice cream machine or freeze until hard for pretty scoops *(p. 6)*.

Earl Grey Tea Ice Cream

When I decided to do a chapter on tea ice creams I naively thought that they would all require the same amount of loose tea. So wrong! I ended up spending more time on each tea ice cream flavor than any of the others in this book! It was well worth it though, because I love them so much.

INGREDIENTS

cashew milk or hemp milk *(p. 3)* · coconut milk *(canned full-fat)* · Earl Grey tea · guar gum *(or other thickener, p. 5)* · honey or raw agave · vanilla extract · water

Add to medium sized pot:
    2¼ cups coconut milk
    1 cup cashew milk or hemp milk
    ¾ cup water
    1 tbsp + 1 tsp Earl Grey tea

Bring to a simmer, watching carefully so it doesn't boil over. Turn off the heat, put the lid on and steep for about 20 minutes. Remove the lid and let the mixture cool. Strain the tea from the liquid.

Add to high power blender or food processor:
    strained liquid
    ½ cup honey or raw agave
    1 tsp vanilla extract
    ½ tsp guar gum
Puree until creamy and smooth.

Freeze for about two hours or refrigerate until cold. Pour into ice cream machine, per manufacturers instructions.

Eat straight from ice cream machine or freeze until hard for pretty scoops *(p. 6)*.

Tea Ice Cream

...tographs of matcha ice cream I was disappointed when mine didn't come ...n. To make yours more green try adding equal parts of yellow and blue ...tural food coloring.

INGREDIENTS

cashew milk or hemp milk *(p. 3)* · coconut milk *(canned full-fat)* · guar gum *(or other thickener, p. 5)* · honey or raw agave · Matcha Green Tea powder *(I use The Republic of Tea, Matcha Stone Ground Green Tea Powder)* · vanilla extract · water ·

Add to medium sized pot:

2¼ cups coconut milk

1 cup cashew milk or hemp milk

¾ cup water

3 tsp Matcha Green Tea powder

Bring to a simmer, watching carefully so it doesn't boil over. Turn off the heat, put the lid on and steep for about 20 minutes. Remove the lid and let the mixture cool. *This powder is not strained like the other teas.*

Add to high power blender or food processor:

liquid tea mixture

½ cup honey or raw agave

1 tsp vanilla extract

½ tsp guar gum

Puree until creamy and smooth.

Freeze for about two hours or refrigerate until cold. Pour into ice cream machine, per manufacturers instructions.

Eat straight from ice cream machine or freeze until hard for pretty scoops *(p. 6)*.

Honeysuckle Tea Ice Cream

Have you ever licked the sweet juice inside a honeysuckle? I have fond memories of pulling the summer honeysuckles apart, and tasting the sweet flavor as a little girl in Maryland. This ice cream flavor takes me back.

INGREDIENTS

cashew milk or hemp milk *(p. 3)* · coconut milk *(canned full-fat)* · guar gum (or *other thickener, p. 5*) · honey or raw agave · honeysuckle white tea *(I use The Republic of Tea, Honeysuckle White Tea)* · vanilla extract · water

Add to medium sized pot:
  2¼ cups coconut milk
  1 cup cashew milk or hemp milk
  ¾ cup water
  2 tsp honeysuckle white tea

Bring to a simmer, watching carefully so it doesn't boil over. Turn off the heat, put the lid on and steep for about 20 minutes. Remove the lid and let the mixture cool. Strain the tea from the liquid.

Add to high power blender or food processor:
  strained liquid
  ½ cup honey or raw agave
  1 tsp vanilla extract
  ½ tsp guar gum
Puree until creamy and smooth.

Freeze for about two hours or refrigerate until cold. Pour into ice cream machine, per manufacturers instructions.

Eat straight from ice cream machine or freeze until hard for pretty scoops *(p. 6)*.

Jasmine Tea Ice Cream

Jasmine is one of the best scents in the world, isn't it? Whenever I'm in a boutique gift shop I can always be caught standing by the jasmine soaps, inhaling deeply with a bar against my nose. This ice cream tastes pretty like jasmine, if that makes any sense.

INGREDIENTS

cashew milk or hemp milk *(p. 3)* · coconut milk *(canned full-fat)* · guar gum *(or other thickener, p. 5)* · honey or raw agave · jasmine white tea *(I use The Republic of Tea, Asian Jasmine White Tea)* · vanilla extract · water

Add to medium sized pot:

    2¼ cups coconut milk

    1 cup cashew milk or hemp milk

    ¾ cup water

    1 tbsp + ½ tsp jasmine white tea

Bring to a simmer, watching carefully so it doesn't boil over. Turn off the heat, put the lid on and steep for about 20 minutes. Remove the lid and let the mixture cool. Strain the tea from the liquid.

Add to high power blender or food processor:

    strained liquid

    ½ cup honey or raw agave

    2 tsp vanilla extract

    ½ tsp guar gum

Puree until creamy and smooth.

Freeze for about two hours or refrigerate until cold. Pour into ice cream machine, per manufacturers instructions.

Eat straight from ice cream machine or freeze until hard for pretty scoops *(p. 6)*.

Rooibos Tea Ice Cream

cashew milk or hemp milk *(p. 3)* · coconut milk *(canned full-fat)* · guar gum *(or other thickener, p. 5)* · honey or raw agave · red rooibos *(I use The Republic of Tea, Double Red Rooibos Tea)* · vanilla extract · water

Add to medium sized pot:

    2¼ cups coconut milk

    1 cup cashew milk or hemp milk

    ¾ cup water

    3 tbsp red rooibos

Bring to a simmer, watching carefully so it doesn't boil over. Turn off the heat, put the lid on and steep for about 20 minutes. Remove the lid and let the mixture cool. Strain the tea from the liquid.

Add to high power blender or food processor:

    strained liquid

    ½ cup honey or raw agave

    1 tsp vanilla extract

    ½ tsp guar gum

Puree until creamy and smooth.

Freeze for about two hours or refrigerate until cold. Pour into ice cream machine, per manufacturers instructions.

Eat straight from ice cream machine or freeze until hard for pretty scoops *(p. 6)*.

Spiced Apple Tea Ice Cream

This is such a great flavor for eating in the fall. Apples, cinnamon, cloves, and orange peel impart all the flavor of mulled cider, but with the added creaminess of ice cream. It makes me want to jump in a pile of dry fall leaves.

apple juice *(with no added sugar)* · cashew milk or hemp milk *(p. 3)* · coconut milk *(canned full-fat)* · guar gum *(or other thickener, p. 5)* · honey or raw agave · mulling spices or cinnamon apple spice herbal tea *(I use R.W.Knudsen Organic Mulling Spices or Celestial Seasonings Cinnamon Apple Spice)* · vanilla extract

Add to medium sized pot:
- 2 cups coconut milk
- 1 cup cashew milk or hemp milk
- 1 cup apple juice
- 1 tbsp mulling spices or cinnamon apple spice herbal tea

Bring to a simmer, watching carefully so it doesn't boil over. Turn off the heat, put the lid on and steep for about 20 minutes. Remove the lid and let the mixture cool. Strain the tea from the liquid.

Add to high power blender or food processor:
- strained liquid
- ½ cup honey or raw agave
- 1 tsp vanilla extract
- ½ tsp guar gum

Optional: yellow India Tree food coloring, to desired color

Puree until creamy and smooth.

Freeze for about two hours or refrigerate until cold. Pour into ice cream machine, per manufacturers instructions.

Eat straight from ice cream machine or freeze until hard for pretty scoops *(p. 6)*.

Spice

Frozen Coffee or Tea Lattes

The frozen tea latte in this photo is chai (p. 38). I chose it for the picture because of its gorgeous brown color. And half the fun of taking the photo is devouring the ice cream afterwards.

INGREDIENTS

your favorite coffee or tea ice cream · coconut milk *(canned full-fat)* · honey or raw agave · vanilla extract

Follow the directions for my Coffee Ice Cream or any tea flavored ice cream.

Add chilled ice cream puree to the ice cream machine. Turn the machine off when you reach milkshake consistency. Pour into glasses. Top with Whipped Coconut Cream

WHIPPED COCONUT CREAM

Place one can of full-fat Thai Kitchen coconut milk in the refrigerator over night. The milk will separate into a thick cream and a liquid.

Add to a small mixing bowl:
 coconut cream from one can of separated
  coconut milk *(do not use the liquid)*
 1 tbsp honey or agave
 1 tsp vanilla extract

Whip with electric mixer for about two minutes. Chill. Whip again before serving.

Optional: To pipe onto frozen lattes (as seen in the photo at right) add whipped coconut cream to one corner of a plastic storage bag. Cut ½ inch off the tip off the bag. Twist the air out of the bag to pipe the whipped coconut cream.

Chai

Ginger Kombucha Tea Ice Cream

At home we make ginger flavored Kombucha by adding some chopped crystallized ginger to the second fermentation. If you don't like the taste of ginger, try using another flavor of Kombucha, and omit the ginger root from the recipe. See www.TheSpunkyCoconut.com for how to make your own Kombucha, and to read the health benefits.

INGREDIENTS

coconut milk *(canned full-fat)* · medjool dates · ginger root · guar gum *(or other thickener, p. 5)* · Kombucha *(I make my own or buy High Country Ginger)* · vanilla extract

Add to high power blender or food processor:
　2 cups ginger kombucha
　½ cup soft pitted medjool dates
Puree until creamy and smooth.

Add:
　1 ½ cups coconut milk
　1 tsp vanilla extract
　1 to 2 inches fresh peeled ginger root
　　(to your taste)
　½ tsp guar gum
Puree until creamy and smooth.

Freeze for about an hour or refrigerate until cold. Pour into ice cream machine, per manufacturers instructions.

Eat straight from ice cream machine or freeze until hard for pretty scoops *(p. 6)*.

CAKE & COOKIES

Brownie Batter Ice Cream

INGREDIENTS

almond butter · applesauce · arrowroot powder · baking soda · Chocolate Ice Cream base *(p. 13)* · cocoa or raw cacao powder · coconut sugar powder *(grind coconut sugar in Magic Bullet or coffee grinder to make powder)* · sea salt · liquid stevia *(p. 4)* · water

BROWNIE BATTER

(based on Best Ever Brownies from my Baked Goods & Desserts cookbook)

Add to bowl:
   ½ cup applesauce
   1 tbsp arrowroot powder
   2 tbsp water
Mix with electric mixer.

Add:
   1 cup almond butter
   ¼ cup plus 3 tbsp cocoa
     or raw cacao powder
   ¼ cup coconut sugar powder
   ⅛ - ¼ tsp liquid stevia *(or omit stevia and double coconut sugar powder)*
   ¼ tsp sea salt
   ½ tsp baking soda
Mix with electric mixer.

CHOCOLATE ICE CREAM

Make Chocolate Ice Cream base.

Freeze for about an hour or refrigerate until cold. Pour into ice cream machine, per manufacturers instructions.

Fold in Brownie Batter. Freeze until hard for pretty scoops *(p. 6)*.

Brownies a la mode

I love brownies a la mode. These brownies are one of my favorites because they meet my philosophy of *even-dessert-can-be-healthy-and-nutrient-dense*. They are high in protein, and low in carbs and sugar. But any brownie recipe you love will work too. For brownies to be eaten as brownie batter see p. 50.

For brownies to be eaten as brownie batter see p. 50.

INGREDIENTS

almond meal flour *(I use Bob's Red Mill)* · baking soda · cocoa powder · dairy-free chocolate chips · coconut milk *(canned full-fat)* · grapeseed oil · honey or raw agave · vanilla liquid stevia *(p. 4)* · cooked white beans · sea salt

vanilla liquid stevia *(p. 4)*

Add to food processor:
- 2 cups cooked white beans
- ¼ cup grapeseed oil
- ¼ cup honey or raw agave
- ¼ cup coconut milk
- ¼ tsp vanilla liquid stevia
- ¼ tsp sea salt
- ½ tsp baking soda

Puree until completely smooth *(about 5 minutes)*.

Add:
- ¼ cup cocoa powder
- ½ cup almond meal flour

Puree about 30 seconds more, scraping the bowl as needed.

Fold in ¼ cup dairy-free chocolate chips. Scoop into a greased square baking dish. Spread evenly. Bake at 325°F for about 35 minutes. Serve warm with a scoop of ice cream on top. Store in the refrigerator. These are also great cold.

Carrot Cake Ice Cream

I'm crazy about carrot cake. I make it so much that I've taken to making it several different ways. Sometimes I make my own carrot cake recipes, sometimes I use my friends recipes. If I could only eat one kind of cake ever again, I would choose carrot cake. It only makes sense that I love this carrot cake ice cream too.

INGREDIENTS

allspice · carrots · cashew milk or hemp milk *(p. 3)* · cinnamon · coconut milk *(canned full-fat)* · guar gum *(or other thickener, p. 5)* · honey or raw agave · raisins · sea salt · walnuts

Chop fresh carrots into ½ inch pieces until you have about 2 cups worth *(about 4 whole carrots)*. Steam the carrots until they are fork-tender *(about 10 minutes)*.

Add to high power blender or food processor:
    steamed carrots from above
    1¼ cups coconut milk
    1 cup cashew milk or hemp milk
    ½ cup honey or raw agave
    2 tsp cinnamon
    ¼ tsp allspice
    ⅛ tsp sea salt
    ½ tsp guar gum
Puree until creamy and smooth.

Freeze for about two hours or refrigerate until cold. Pour into ice cream machine, per manufacturers instructions.

Add 1 cup raisins and 1 cup chopped walnuts to ice cream when it is soft serve consistency.

Eat straight from ice cream machine or freeze until hard for pretty scoops *(p. 6)*.

Chocolate Chip Cookies

INGREDIENTS

almond meal flour *(I use Bob's Red Mill)* · apple cider vinegar · applesauce · baking powder · baking soda · chia seed meal *(I grind my seeds in a coffee grinder or Magic Bullet)* · dairy-free chocolate chips *(I use Enjoy Life)* · coconut flour · honey or coconut sugar · grapeseed oil or coconut oil · sea salt · vanilla extract

COOKIE DOUGH

Add to bowl:
- ½ cup applesauce
- 2 tbsp chia seed meal *(double if substituting with flax seed meal)*
- 1 tbsp apple cider vinegar*
- ¼ cup honey or coconut sugar
- ¼ cup grapeseed oil or coconut oil, liquefied
- ¼ tsp sea salt
- 2 tsp vanilla extract

Mix with electric mixer.

Add:
- 1 cup almond meal flour
- ½ cup coconut flour *(plus more as needed)*
- 1 tsp baking soda
- 1 tsp baking powder
   (see TheSpunkyCoconut.com for a grain-free baking powder recipe)
- ⅓ cup dairy-free chocolate chips

Mix again.

BAKED COOKIES

Roll a few balls of dough in your hands then flatten and bake for cookies to garnish cookie dough ice cream. Bake at 350°F for about 15 minutes, depending on the size of your cookies.

*Note: baking soda and vinegar create a slight rise in egg-free recipes. However, you may omit the vinegar if you plan on eating the dough raw.

Chocolate Chip Cookie Dough Ice Cream

INGREDIENTS

Chocolate Chip Cookie dough *(p. 54)* · Vanilla Ice Cream base *(p. 34)*

Make Chocolate Chip Cookie dough.

Make Vanilla Ice Cream base.

Freeze for about an hour or refrigerate until cold. Pour into ice cream machine, per manufacturers instructions.

Fold in chunks of cookie dough. Eat right away or freeze until hard for pretty scoops *(p. 6)*.

Chocolate Chip
Ice Cream Sandwiches

INGREDIENTS
Vanilla Ice Cream base *(p. 34)* · Double batch of Chocolate Chip Cookie Dough *(p. 54)*

Make Vanilla Ice Cream base.

Make a double batch of Chocolate Chip
Cookie Dough.

Use flour to roll out the dough. I like to make
8 big circles, about ½ inch thick, for 4 big ice
cream sandwiches. I use a 32 ounce (1 quart)
mason jar lid as a cookie cutter. It's about 3½
inches wide.

Bake at 350°F for about 15 minutes, depending
on the size of your cookies. Cool the cookies
on wire racks then freeze them before adding
the ice cream *(this just makes them easier to
assemble)*. If the ice cream is frozen hard, allow
it to soften on the counter for 20 minutes or
more as needed. Add a scoop of softened vanilla
ice cream to the bottom size of a cookie. Press
another cookie down on top. Eat right away or
freeze for later.

Chocolate Chocolate Ice Cream Sandwiches

The great thing about the cookies and cookie doughs in this book is that they are all egg-free in addition to grain-free.

INGREDIENTS

almond meal *(I use Bob's Red Mill)* · applesauce *(with no added sugar)* · baking soda · chia seed meal *(I grind my seeds in a coffee grinder or Magic Bullet)* · cocoa powder · Chocolate Ice Cream base *(p. 13)* · coconut sugar · mint extract · tapioca flour · vanilla liquid stevia *(p. 4)*

Make Chocolate Ice Cream base.
Make Chocolate Cookies, recipe follows:

CHOCOLATE COOKIES

Add to a small bowl:

- ½ cup applesauce with no added sugar
- ¼ to ½ tsp vanilla liquid stevia *(depending on how sweet you want them)*
- 2 tbsp chia seed meal
- *Optional:* ½ tsp mint extract

Mix with electric mixer.

In a separate bowl combine:

- 3 cups almond meal
- ½ cup cocoa powder
- ¼ cup tapioca flour
- ¼ cup coconut sugar
- 1 tsp baking soda

Combine the dry and wet ingredients with an electric mixer until the batter gets all sticky. Scoop your dough onto unbleached parchment paper. Flour the top if necessary and roll out the dough.

Cut 12 squares to make 6 cookies. Cookie cutters would work too (and the kids can pick their own shape). Bake at 350°F degrees for about 15 minutes. Cool the cookies on wire racks then freeze them before adding the ice cream (*this just makes them easier to assemble*).

If the ice cream is frozen hard, allow it to soften on the counter for 20 minutes or more as needed. Add a scoop of softened vanilla ice cream to the bottom size of a cookie. Press another cookie down on top. Eat right away or freeze for later.

Gingerbread Cookies

allspice · almond meal flour *(I use Bob's Red Mill)* · applesauce *(with no added sweetener)* · baking soda · cinnamon · coconu flour · coconut sugar powder *(grind coconut sugar in Magic Bullet or coffee grinder to make powder)* · flax seed meal or chia seed meal *(I grind my seeds in a coffee grinder or Magic Bullet)* · grapeseed oil or coconut oil · ground ginger · vanilla extract

COOKIE DOUGH

Add to bowl:
- ½ cup applesauce
- 3 tbsp flax seed meal
  OR 2 tbsp chia seed meal
- 1 tsp vanilla extract
- ½ cup coconut sugar powder
- ¼ cup grapeseed oil or coconut oil, liquefied
- ¼ tsp allspice
- 1½ tsp cinnamon
- 1½ tsp ground ginger

Mix with electric mixer.

Add:
- 1 cup almond meal flour
- ½ cup coconut flour, sifted
- 1 tsp baking soda

Mix with electric mixer.

BAKED COOKIES

Roll a few balls of dough in your hands then flatten and bake for cookies to garnish. Bake at 350°F for about 15 minutes, depending on the size of your cookies.

Gingerbread Cookie Dough Ice Cream

Like my chocolate chip cookie dough, I eat this gingerbread cookie dough by the spoonful. When I was working on new ice creams for this book I wanted to have more than one dough or batter flavor, quite selfishly. Plus, having flavors that suit the season makes it even more fun.

INGREDIENTS

Gingerbread Cookie dough *(p. 59)* · Vanilla Ice Cream base *(p. 34)*

Make Gingerbread Cookie dough.

Make Vanilla Ice Cream base.

Add to Vanilla Ice Cream base:
   1½ tsp cinnamon
   1 tsp ground ginger
   pinch of allspice
Puree until creamy and smooth.

Freeze for about one hour or refrigerate until cold. Pour into ice cream machine, per manufacturers instructions.

Fold in chunks of Gingerbread Cookie dough. Eat right away or freeze until hard for pretty scoops *(p. 6)*.

YOGURT, POPS & SHERBET

Yummy Yogurt Drink

I am completely obsessed with my dairy-free yogurt and yogurt drink. I make it constantly. The beauty of making frozen yogurt is that you can leave out the thickener (gelatin or agar powder for vegan) that you would add for yogurt, and make a yogurt drink instead. It's so fast and easy. The only hard part is waiting while it does its magic.

cashew milk · *(p. 3)* · coconut milk *(canned full-fat)* · coconut sugar · contents of dairy-free probiotic capsules · vanilla liquid stevia *(p. 4)*

Add to a large pot:

    4 cups coconut milk

    4 cups cashew milk

    2 tbsp coconut sugar

    ⅛ to ¼ tsp vanilla liquid stevia (to your taste)

Bring to simmer, watching carefully so it doesn't boil over. Simmer for about one minute. Turn off heat and let cool.

When the thermometer reads about 92°F whisk in the contents of enough dairy-free probiotic capsules to equal about 37 billion.

Transfer to a large glass container with a lid. Set aside. Sandwich a heating pad between two kitchen towels on the counter. Place the yogurt in the glass container on top of the towel-covered heating pad, with the lid on. Use low to medium heat. It should make the bottom of the container warm, but not hot.

The yogurt drink will be ready to refrigerate in 12 to 24 hours, or when it tastes to your liking. This makes 8 cups of yogurt drink, which is enough for several batches of frozen yogurt. We like to make a lot so we can drink it too. Cut the recipe in half if you prefer to make less.

Optional: For yogurt making instructions see www.TheSpunkyCoconut.com under the label "Yogurt & Granola".

Note: I've tried this with other milk-substitutes, like hemp milk, and didn't like the results. Cashew and coconut milk work best.

Apricot Amaretto Frozen Yogurt

INGREDIENTS

amaretto extract *(I use Olive Nation, Pure Amaretto Extract)* · apricot nectar *(I use Bionaturae, Organic Apricot Nectar)* · guar gum *(or other thickener, p. 5)* · honey or raw agave · Yummy Yogurt Drink *(p. 62)*

Add to high power blender or food processor:

2¼ cups Yummy Yogurt Drink or
store-bought dairy-free yogurt

1¼ cups apricot nectar

¼ cup honey or raw agave

¼ tsp amaretto extract

½ tsp guar gum

Puree until creamy and smooth.

Freeze for about an hour or refrigerate
until cold. Pour into ice cream machine, per
manufacturers instructions.

Eat straight from ice cream machine or freeze
until hard for pretty scoops *(p. 6)*.

Lemon Lime Frozen Yogurt

INGREDIENTS

coconut water *(I use Amy & Brian)* · guar gum *(or other thickener, p. 5)* · honey or raw agave · lemon juice · lemon zest or lime zest · lime juice · sea salt · vanilla extract · Yummy Yogurt Drink *(p. 62)*

Add to high power blender or food processor:

2 cups Yummy Yogurt Drink or
    store-bought dairy-free yogurt
1¼ cups coconut water
½ cup honey or raw agave
1 tbsp lemon juice
1 tbsp lime juice
1 tsp vanilla extract
½ to 1 tsp lemon zest or lime zest *(as desired)*
pinch of sea salt
½ tsp guar gum

Puree until creamy and smooth.

Freeze for about an hour or refrigerate until cold. Pour into ice cream machine, per manufacturers instructions.

Eat straight from ice cream machine or freeze until hard for pretty scoops *(p. 6)*.

Lemon & Lime

Orange Cream Frozen Yogurt

INGREDIENTS
guar gum *(or other thickener, p. 5)* · honey or raw agave · oranges · vanilla extract ·
Yummy Yogurt Drink *(p. 62)*

Add to high power blender or food processor:

3 oranges, peeled and seeded *(about 2 cups)*

2 cups Yummy Yogurt Drink or
store-bought dairy-free yogurt

¼ cup honey or raw agave

1 tsp vanilla extract

½ tsp guar gum

Puree until creamy and smooth.

Freeze for about an hour or refrigerate
until cold. Pour into ice cream machine, per
manufacturers instructions.

Eat straight from ice cream machine or freeze
until hard for pretty scoops *(p. 6)*.

Peach Frozen Yogurt

coconut water *(I use Amy & Brian)* · guar gum *(or other thickener, p. 5)* · honey or raw agave · lemon juice · peaches · peach nectar *(I use Bionaturae)* · vanilla extract

Add to high power blender or food processor:

    10 ounces peaches *(about 2½ cups)*

    2 cups Yummy Yogurt Drink *(p. 62)* or
       store-bought dairy-free yogurt

    ½ cup coconut water or peach nectar

    ⅓ cup honey or raw agave

    1 tsp lemon juice

    1 tsp vanilla extract

    ½ tsp guar gum

Puree until creamy and smooth.

Freeze for about an hour or refrigerate
until cold. Pour into ice cream machine, per
manufacturers instructions.

Eat straight from ice cream machine or freeze
until hard for pretty scoops *(p. 6)*.

Almond & Chocolate Protein Pudding Pops

To Zoe and Ashley these pudding pops are tied with grape sorbet for their favorite recipe in this book. Made with almond butter, protein powder and chia seeds, they are incredibly nutrient-dense, and often eaten as breakfast. You can substitute cocoa powder for the raw cacao powder, but don't. Raw cacao has more magnesium than any other food, and the majority of us are deficient in it.

INGREDIENTS

almond butter · chia seeds *(grind them first using a coffee grinder or Magic Bullet if you don't have a Blendtec or Vitamix—otherwise the pops wont be smooth)* · honey or raw agave · vanilla protein powder *(our favorite is Vitol Egg Protein, which is not vegan)* · raw cacao powder · water

Add to high power blender or food processor:

    2 cups water

    1 cup almond butter

    ¼ cup honey or raw agave

    ¼ cup raw cacao powder

    ¼ cup of your favorite vanilla protein powder

    ¼ cup chia seeds

Pour into molds.

Makes 6 large pops.

Note: To remove the pops from the mold: Place the pops in a bowl of very hot water for as much time as needed to loosen them.

Cherry & Yogurt Pops

INGREDIENTS
frozen cherries · honey or raw agave · Yummy Yogurt Drink *(p. 62)*

Pulse 2 cups thawed cherries and 2 tablespoon honey or raw agave in a high power blender or food processor. Set aside. Add a couple tablespoons of Yummy Yogurt Drink or store-bought dairy-free yogurt to the pop molds. Add a couple tablespoons of the pulsed cherries. Continue layering until the molds are full. Add the sticks and freeze.

Note: To remove the pops from the mold: Place the pops in a bowl of very hot water for as much time as needed to loosen them.

Chocolate Chip Banana Bread Pudding Pops

INGREDIENTS

almond butter · bananas · dairy-free chocolate chips *(I use Enjoy Life because they're mini)* · coconut milk *(canned full-fat)* · Earth Balance Buttery Spread *(I use soy-free)* · honey or raw agave · lemon juice · sea salt

Place large pan over low/medium heat. Cut 4 bananas into ¾ inch pieces. Saute banana pieces in 2 tbsp Earth Balance Buttery Spread about 3 minutes per side, or until golden brown.

Add to high power blender or food processor:
  sauteed bananas and Earth Balance from
    the pan
  1 tbsp lemon juice
  1 cup coconut milk
  ½ cup water
  ¼ cup almond butter
  2 tbsp honey or raw agave
  ⅛ tsp sea salt
Puree.

Fold in ¼ cup dairy-free chocolate chips

Pour into molds.

Makes a little more than 6 large pops.

Note: To remove the pops from the mold: Place the pops in a bowl of very hot water for as much time as needed to loosen them.

Chocolate Covered Kiwi & Banana Pops

INGREDIENTS

bananas · coconut oil · dairy-free chocolate *(I use Chocolove 70%)* · kiwi

Peel 3 kiwi and cut each in half. Insert a lollipop stick lengthwise into the kiwi halves *(I get lollipop sticks at the craft store)*. Lay them down in a large rectangular baking dish, lined with unbleached parchment paper.

Peel 1 or 2 bananas. Cut into about 1 inch pieces. Add 3 cut pieces lengthwise to a lollipop stick. Lay them in the dish with the kiwi sticks.

Put the lid on the dish (or cover with plastic) and freeze overnight.

Melt over a double boiler:
  2 bars dark dairy-free chocolate, or
    about 6½ oz
  ¼ cup coconut oil

Cool for about five minutes then add to a tall skinny glass. Dip the frozen banana pops first, while the chocolate sauce is deep enough to cover all 3 pieces. Let chocolate drip off over the glass. Hold for a few seconds until the chocolate is dry, then lay them back in the large rectangular baking dish. Dip the kiwi pops next, letting the chocolate dry before laying them down. Store covered in the freezer.

Thaw for about ten minutes before eating.

Save the leftover chocolate mixture in a mason jar in the refrigerator. Reheat for more chocolate covered kiwi & banana pops, or pour over scoops of ice cream *(as seen on p. 37)*.

Watermelon Fruit Pops

These pretty fruit pops are naturally red from watermelon puree.

INGREDIENTS
banana · blueberries · kiwi · watermelon

Add to high power blender or food processor:
   About 2 cups fresh watermelon chunks
     (removing as many seeds as possible)
Puree.

Add to each pop mold:
   two slices of peeled kiwi
   defrosted blueberries
   two slices of banana
   more blueberries between the banana
     and kiwi slices to press them against the
     walls of the mold

Fill with watermelon puree. Add the sticks
and freeze.

Note: To remove the pops from the mold: Place
the pops in a bowl of very hot water for as much
time as needed to loosen them.

Coconut Water Sherbet

The dates will make this sherbet a light khaki color. You can use honey or agave if you prefer, but the dates make it less icy.

INGREDIENTS

coconut milk *(canned full-fat)* · coconut water *(I use Amy & Brian)* · medjool dates · guar gum *(or other thickener, p. 5)* · lemon juice or lime juice

Add to high power blender or food processor:
- 2½ cups coconut water
- 1 cup coconut milk
- 2 tsp lemon juice or lime juice
- ½ cup soft pitted medjool dates
- ½ tsp guar gum

Puree until creamy and smooth.

Freeze for about an hour or refrigerate until cold. Pour into ice cream machine, per manufacturers instructions.

Eat straight from ice cream machine or freeze until hard for pretty scoops *(p. 6)*.

Grape Sorbet

My sorbets were very icy when I first started making them, partly because sorbet doesn't contain any milk. While the kids loved them this way, I really didn't. Then I began experimenting with adding dates and guar gum. Voila! These sorbets are so nice and soft, they hardly take any time to defrost before you can scoop them. You can substitute a quarter cup of honey or agave plus one ripe banana, which will also give you a fabulous texture, if you like a little banana flavor.

INGREDIENTS

coconut water *(I use Amy & Brian)* · medjool dates · grape juice *(I use R.W. Knudsen, Organic Just Concord)* · guar gum *(or other thickener, p. 5)* · lemon juice

Add to high power blender or food processor:
- ½ cup soft pitted medjool dates
- 2½ cups grape juice
- ½ cup coconut water
- 1 tsp lemon juice
- ½ tsp guar gum

Puree until creamy and smooth.

Freeze for about an hour or refrigerate until cold. Pour into ice cream machine, per manufacturers instructions.

Eat straight from ice cream machine or freeze until hard for pretty scoops *(p. 6)*.

Pomegranate Sorbet

You can make these sorbets with any flavor of juice you like, but pomegranate and grape are our favorites.

INGREDIENTS

coconut water *(I use Amy & Brian)* · medjool dates · guar gum *(or other thickener, p. 5)* · lemon juice · pomegranate juice *(I use R.W. Knudsen Just Pomegranate)*

Add to high power blender or food processor:
   ½ cup soft pitted medjool dates
   2½ cups pomegranate juice
   ½ cup coconut water
   1 tsp lemon juice
   ½ tsp guar gum
Puree until creamy and smooth.

Freeze for about an hour or refrigerate
until cold. Pour into ice cream machine, per
manufacturers instructions.

Eat straight from ice cream machine or freeze
until hard for pretty scoops *(p. 6)*.

Strawberry Rhubarb Sherbet

*One day I was testing recipes for this book, when I looked into my freezer and saw frozen rhubarb. My husband, who **loves** my strawberry rhubarb pie was standing nearby. "I have an awesome idea," I said to him, wide-eyed, "Strawberry rhubarb sherbet." (Only I pronounced it "sherbert" with a second "r," because that's how everyone says it where I'm from.) Andrew literally jumped with excitement at the idea. We hope you love it too.*

INGREDIENTS

cashew milk or hemp milk *(p. 3)* · cinnamon · coconut milk *(canned full-fat)* · guar gum *(or other thickener, p. 5)* · honey or raw agave · lemon juice · rhubarb · sea salt · strawberries · vanilla extract

Add to a medium sized pot:
    about 3 cups rhubarb (or 10 ounces)
    about 2 cups strawberries (or
        about 10 ounces)
    ½ cup honey or raw agave
    ⅛ tsp sea salt
Simmer with the lid on, but slightly cracked for about 15 minutes.

Add to high power blender or food processor:
    the cooked strawberries and rhubarb, plus
        all of the liquids in the pot.
    1 cup cashew milk or hemp milk
    ½ cup coconut milk
    2 tsp lemon juice
    1 tsp vanilla extract
    1 tsp cinnamon
    ½ tsp guar gum

Puree until creamy and smooth.

Freeze for about two hours or refrigerate until cold. Pour into ice cream machine, per manufacturers instructions.

Eat straight from ice cream machine or freeze until hard for pretty scoops *(p. 6)*.

(Pictured with brownies from p. 51)

16101937R00049

Made in the USA
Lexington, KY
05 July 2012